# HOW TO TRAIN MY PUPPY!

## PUPPY CARE BOOK FOR KIDS
## CHILDREN'S DOG BOOKS

**petsunchained**
**(PETS & ANIMALS)**

Speedy Publishing LLC
40 E. Main St. #1156
Newark, DE 19711
www.speedypublishing.com
Copyright 2017

In this book, we're going to talk all about how to train your new puppy. So, let's get right to it!

**Y**ou've chosen a new puppy and now you're going to bring her or him home with you. A new puppy will be a lot of responsibility, but it will be a lot of fun too!

# PREPARING YOUR HOME FOR A NEW PUPPY

Before you bring your new pet home, take a careful look around your house. You want to get down to the puppy's level and make sure there's nothing that could fall on your new pet or any nooks or crannies where it could get stuck. Puppies sometimes love to chew so make sure there are no electrical cords that your puppy might be able to access.

You should go outdoors and make sure that there's a fenced-in area for your puppy to play. Make sure there are no holes or places where your puppy can dig out and escape.

**A**sk the breeder to give you a piece of the bed that your pet was sleeping on or bring your new bed to the breeder so that he or she can place the litter of puppies there for a day or two before you bring your puppy home. At 8 weeks or so of age, puppies are ready to take home for pets, but scent is important to them. If they can smell the scents of their litter, they'll be more comfortable until they get used to their new environment.

# A SPACE FOR YOUR PUPPY

**P**uppies like to have a space of their own. A cage might seem too confining to you, but it can be a cozy puppy den if you set it up right. It's reassuring to your puppy to be able to see where you are.

A cage or playpen makes toilet training and obedience training much simpler. Make sure that the cage doesn't have any sharp wire. You don't want your puppy's fur or paws to get caught. Your puppy should be able to easily stand up and turn around.

If you have enough space to do this in your home, one of the best arrangements is a cage inside a playpen. That way, you can leave the cage open and the puppy is free to go in and out, but is still enclosed in the playpen. The puppy's bedding should be positioned inside the cage.

Your pet's water and food bowl and pee pads will be arranged inside the playpen but outside the cage. After your puppy eats, make sure he or she stays in the playpen so the pee pad or litter box can be used. Once your puppy is potty trained, your new pet can have the run of the house.

The first night your puppy is without the scent of its mother and siblings is a little frightening. If you can, you might want to sleep near your puppy's enclosure so he or she can smell you and lick your hand for reassurance. If you can't do that, a night light or a clock that sounds like a heartbeat will help your puppy go off to sleep.

# FEEDING YOUR PUPPY

**Y**our new puppy is energetic and super hungry! Puppies have different needs than adult dogs because of their rapid growth. Your puppy should already be weaned from its mother's milk from about 8 weeks old. At the breeder or shelter where you got your puppy, it was eating a specific type of food, so it might be good to stick with that same type until you have time to consult the vet.

**A**fter your new pet has been home for about a week, you can call the veterinarian to ask for advice about any new diet regimens. The labeling on most food for dogs gives you the requirements for what your puppy should be eating.

After your puppy has been eating at your home for a month, assess its health. Your pet should be energetic and playful. Your puppy should have a coat that's thick and shiny. Its poop should be well formed and brown because that indicates that your pet is absorbing the proper amount of nutrients.

Your puppy should have meals three times a day until he or she is 6 months old, then after that the growth spurt slows down so feeding twice a day works fine.

**M**ake sure your pet has fresh water available all the time. At the start, you can expect your puppy to poop within a half hour of eating. This will help you to plan so you can take your puppy outdoors to eliminate accidents until your puppy is housetrained.

**A**t about 4-6 months old, your puppy will lose its baby teeth and get its permanent adult teeth. At this point your puppy will need to chew raw, meaty bones to help during teething. Make sure the bones you provide are raw and not cooked.

You can offer your puppy some natural foods like raw, diced-up lamb, but be sure to clear this with your vet. Don't ever offer your puppy food that you eat. There are lots of human foods that can cause severe health problems for your pet.

# MAKING SURE YOUR PUPPY GETS EXERCISE

Your new puppy wants to run, leap, jump, and play with you. Every breed of puppy needs a different amount of exercise. Some puppies require a more demanding routine than others. Make sure you consult your vet to find out what he or she says about your puppy's exercise routine.

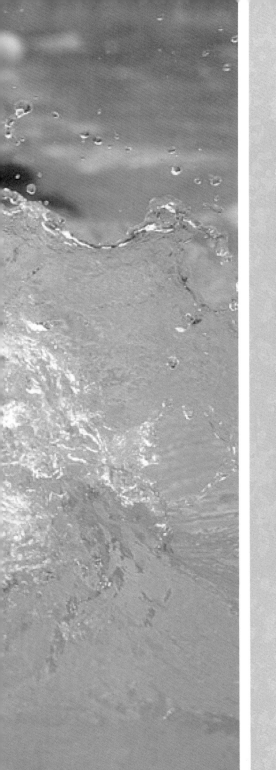

At the beginning, you can start with two 10-15 minute exercise sessions daily. A quick walk in the morning and a game of fetch the ball in the afternoon is one possible idea, but you can do something a little different every day to keep it interesting for your pet. Swimming in a pool with a low-level of water is great exercise for your puppy, but be sure your breed can swim because some breeds don't swim well or at all.

Make sure your puppy is on a leash when you go for outdoor walks. A squirrel or a cat can distract your pet and before you know it your new pet has been lost in the bushes. If your pet is tired or panting a lot, it might be too hot outdoors for a comfortable exercise session.

# BASIC POTTY TRAINING

The most important thing when training your new puppy to go potty is to be consistent. If you have your puppy's cage and playpen set up, your new pet will quickly get used to using the pee pads. Find an area of your yard for a potty spot. It should be free of holes or debris. Take your puppy out to this same spot every time. That way your pet will associate this place as the place to "go potty."

**S**niffing, whining, and pacing are clues that your pet needs to go poop. When you get to the potty spot, use a simple phrase like "go potty" or "toilet time." Your pet will associate that phrase with the act of eliminating so say the same thing every time. Once your puppy has eliminated, give him or her a pat or a special treat so your pet knows that he or she has pleased you. Before you know it, your puppy will be housebroken.

# BASIC SOCIALIZATION

**M**ost puppy behavior problems can be avoided if your pet is properly "socialized" from the start. This essentially means that you want your new pet to get used to sounds, sights, and smells of human environments.

**Y**ou'll want your pet to get used to:

- Handling, such as having a leash put on
- Sounds, such as the vacuum cleaner or dishwasher
- People, such as people with facial hair or people in wheelchairs
- Events, such as visits to the vet or walks in the park
- Other animals, such as other pets or outdoor animals
- Sights, such as remote control toys or umbrellas opening
- Toys, such as balls and Frisbees
- Walking surfaces, such as grass or concrete

**W**hen getting your puppy used to all these new sights and sounds, it helps to have two people. One person can hold the puppy and the other can give treats for good behavior during the event. When you first start this type of training, give a treat at the beginning and at the end of a specific event. Eventually, you can just give a treat when your puppy is calm during any handling session.

Three or four minutes is usually a long enough time period to introduce something new and have your puppy associate that new event with a treat.

# GROOMING

**D**o you remember the first time you had to go to the dentist and how scared you were? This may be the way your new puppy approaches grooming. Once again, consistency matters. Pick the same spot for grooming all the time. You'll be grooming your puppy for the first time when it's about 4 months old. Place your pet on a rubber mat for traction.

Let your puppy smell the new brush and comb and play with them a little. Brush your puppy's coat just a few times and then reward your pet by praising him or her. Do this every day and increase the number of brush strokes daily and after a week or two, your puppy will be used to the grooming routine.

# TAKE GOOD CARE OF YOUR PUPPY!

You're bringing home a new puppy. It's an exciting event! Before you bring your new pet home, you should make sure you know how to feed, exercise, potty train, groom, and socialize your new pet. Having a puppy is a big responsibility, but it's a lot of fun too!

**A**wesome! Now that you've read about how to train your new puppy you may want to read facts about dogs and puppies in the Pets Unchained book Big Dogs & Puppy Facts for Kids | Dogs Book for Children | Children's Dog Books.